Contents

Summary

Improvement in the quality of health and care services depends on good-quality analytical support. We need to use data to identify areas of poor care, guide choices about priorities for care, improve efficiency and improve patient care. An organisation's analytical capability is their ability to analyse information and use it to make decisions. However, we know that in practice health and care systems are often not able to draw on high-quality analytical support. There is a shortage of people with the right skills and tools to do analysis, and collaborate with clinicians and managers on using their insights to improve care. This is exacerbated when the analysts we do have spend much of their time doing relatively low-value work – for example, compiling reports that aren't read. By investing in the analytical workforce, we will be able to unlock the full potential of data.

Better analysis is needed to support:

- clinical decision-making to help busy clinicians diagnose and manage disease

- innovation and change in the NHS, and to evaluate the success of new models of care and whether changes deliver the expected benefits

- effective board-level oversight of complex organisations and care systems

- better everyday management of the monitoring and improvement of the quality and efficiency of care

- senior decision-makers to respond better to national incentives and regulation

- the allocation of finite resources

- better understanding of how patients flow through the system

- new data and digital tools

- patients and the public in using information.

Advances in digital technologies have the potential to transform how care is delivered, but many of these benefits will not be fully realised by organisations without in-house analytical support. The current analyst workforce needs to develop its skill sets and be given leadership and support at senior levels in each organisation.

To get the most out of digital technologies, we need to recognise the importance of investing in the people who shape the information that is communicated and used. Though specialist academic, data-science roles are welcome, we also need people who can implement innovation. Where there has been investment in wider analytics (people, education, tools and techniques), there have been some favourable outcomes, as shown by the examples included in this report.

The challenge of developing analytical capability is not new. However, it is becoming ever more important as new data streams and tools emerge and opportunities for better analysis are missed.

We suggest action is needed at all levels of the system:

- National and local agencies should recognise the development of analytical capability as an important issue. They need to develop local strategies and new ways of working that support the development of the analytical teams in their organisations and identify key gaps.

- Investment in training and development tools to support better analysis is needed. A particular focus should be placed on developing in-house teams. Such development needs to apply not just to analysts but also to clinicians and managers and should encourage good links between the use of analysis and its application.

- The slow uptake of technologies such as open-source software, and techniques such as data-science and operational research, is of concern. These technologies and techniques can bring significant insight and value to health care services but are not being fully exploited at present.

- The sharing of skills and experience across organisations should be supported, to build a culture of 'build it once, share it to everyone'. The analytical community can be fragmented, with limited opportunity for teams to share learning or access specialist skills.

- As much emphasis should be placed on the application and translation of ideas as on their research and development. Investment in new digital technologies and in data-science methods needs accompanying investment in the local analytical workforce.

- The importance of the people who can make sense of data should be recognised, and investment made in the leadership of analytical roles, for instance by having a Chief Analytical Officer in each organisation.

- Most importantly, we need to set higher standards for the way information is used in delivering care and recognise the full potential of the datasets already held.

Introduction

'One of the greatest opportunities of the 21st century is the potential to safely harness the power of the technology revolution, which has transformed our society, to meet the challenges of improving health and providing better, safer, sustainable care for all.'
National Information Board[1]

The ability to exploit advances in digital technology in support of better health and better health care is a priority for health care services.[2] *The NHS Long Term Plan,*[3] published in January 2019, envisages a central role for technology, forecasting that technology will empower people, support health and care professionals to deliver better care, improve clinical efficiency and safety and improve population health overall. Alongside service innovations such as digital-first primary care and the NHS App, there are plans to create better digital infrastructure and build a digital-ready workforce that can make effective use of technologies as they are developed. This approach to digital infrastructure largely consists of the adoption of technology standards, to ensure that data are accessible and that it is possible for different systems to exchange information, and an expansion of the number of acute, mental health and ambulance trusts working with the NHS Global Digital Exemplars on information technology (IT) projects.

All these initiatives involve data, which the NHS has in abundance. A digital footprint is generated almost every time a person comes into contact with a service (Box 1). The volume of data will continue to grow as the NHS spends billions of pounds on its information systems. However, it is failing to make the most of the benefits that can flow from these systems, because there are not enough people with the right skills to use the information that is being collected.

Box 1: The volume of electronic information in NHS health care systems is growing

- It has been estimated that as much as 30% of the entire world's stored data is generated in health care systems. A single patient can typically generate close to 80MB of data each year in imaging and electronic medical record data.[4]
- NHS services see 1 million patients every 36 hours.[5] Almost all interactions generate some form of electronic record or footprint. There are 200 different data collection systems across health care systems.[6]
- A typical hospital stay requires the collection of several hundred individual data items.
- A GP holds electronic records of every consultation, in coded form, stretching back decades.
- 20 million pieces of patient feedback have been received through the Friends and Family Test alone.
- Increasingly, individuals themselves are generating data about their own health, using apps and websites.

Strategies aimed at exploiting the promise of data typically cover:

- innovation and investment in new technologies

- managing and accessing new data streams in new ways

- investing in the analytical workforce, which can use the data to provide actionable insight.

The third aspect tends to get the least attention – it is less glamorous and solutions are often challenging and long term. But it is an essential requirement if we are to exploit the advantages that new technologies offer.

This report explores some of the ways in which good data analytics can support decision-makers. It also identifies some missed opportunities that flow from our limited ability to make sense of information relevant to health and health care. It is based on the Health Foundation's experience of promoting innovative data analytics in health and social care. One of our projects in this area is the Advancing Applied Analytics programme, which is now supporting 23 teams to improve analytical capability in health and care services.[*]

Better use of patient data can improve the quality and operational efficiency of health care in various ways (Table 1). However, as we discovered in previous work, health and care organisations often have problems accessing analytical skills when needed.[7] For that work, we interviewed people across health and care systems in the UK, and many highlighted the problem of not having the right people to interpret the data and provide useful analysis to clinicians and managers (Box 2). This problem is not new or unique to health services. But it is a serious challenge if we want to make the most of the information collected and realise the benefits of investment in digital technology. Part of the answer is making sure that health care services have in place the systems designers, training and infrastructure necessary for new technology. It also means having people and teams who can help make sense of the growing mountains of data.[8]

Table 1: Information and intelligence provided by data analysts – who it is for and how it is applied

Audience	Examples
General population	• Identifying information sources that might be useful to patients. • Testing the effects of different presentation styles aimed at patients and the general population. • Looking at the effects of new information systems.
All users of health and care services	• Designing and testing the effects of new approaches to sharing information with service users.
Clinical teams	• Developing decision aids/tools that use data to help diagnose or manage diseases (eg risk scores and algorithms). • Informing the design of improvement initiatives. • Monitoring the quality of care delivered over time.

---

[*] For further details, see www.health.org.uk/funding-and-partnerships/programmes/advancing-applied-analytics

Service managers		
	•	Identifying service objectives and monitoring tools (performance indicators).
	•	Tracking new care initiatives and providing the information required to improve them.
	•	Devising and adapting mathematical modelling tools (eg to improve scheduling or patient flow).
	•	Synthesising and summarising the literature on the effectiveness of new interventions and service models.
	•	Supporting data collection and analysis of clinical audits.
Commissioners and planners		
	•	Assessing needs and priorities.
	•	Reviewing evidence of effectiveness and efficiency of service delivery.
	•	Assessing need and demand and forecasting for populations.
	•	Modelling capacity requirements and business planning.
	•	Agreeing evaluation frameworks and monitoring effects of service models.
	•	Monitoring the quality of services.
Those running organisations		
	•	Performance analysis.
	•	Assessment of the economic impacts of changes (eg new technology).
	•	Quality monitoring.
	•	Assessing probable effects of changes before they are made (eg closure of A&E departments).
	•	Forecasting demand for services (eg ahead of winter).
	•	Business and strategic planning.
System- and national-level decision-makers		
	•	Monitoring against strategic priorities.
	•	Developing and applying mathematical models to inform policy (eg vaccination or urgent care).
	•	Regulation of efficiency and quality.
	•	Resource allocation.
	•	Programme evaluation so that the NHS can learn from experience and improve.

This report has been written at a critical moment for the NHS workforce, with over 100,000 vacancies reported by trusts and problems attracting, retaining and motivating staff.[9] Overcoming these wider problems is crucial to building analytical capability in the NHS. But it is equally important to recognise that analytical capability requires its own strategy, one that articulates clear roles for analytical teams in the health care system, as well as leadership models and approaches to supporting collaboration between analysts, clinicians and managers.

Box 2: Issues limiting analytical capability in health care organisations

Analyst numbers and priorities
- In some areas, there are not enough analysts.
- However, the existing workforce is not always used to its full potential.

Analyst skills
- Some analytical teams cannot easily access people with skills in more academic disciplines, such as statistics and economics.
- Analysts need good communication skills and the ability to explain complex ideas to senior managers clearly and concisely.

Access to data and tools
- Lack of the right data can hamper the analysis.
- Better software tools can free up analysts' time from mundane tasks.
- Obtaining data at the right level that satisfies information governance requirements can be challenging.

Professional and personal development
- Analysts often lack opportunities to progress their career to a senior level while still being an analyst.

Fragmentation and isolation
- The ability to share experiences and learn new methods and techniques is essential, but health care analysts can become isolated, working as individuals or in small teams across several organisations.

Senior management recognition
- Senior managers might not always see the need for or value of analytics.

Analytical leadership
- Good leaders – people who understand the supply side of the issues and can also engage with managers at the highest levels – are important.

Adapted from Understanding analytical capability in health care: Do we have more data than insight?[7]

Why should we invest in analytical capability?

'The failure to use information properly in health and care means people can experience unnecessary levels of preventable ill health. Those using services can suffer harm when it could be avoided, could live in greater pain and distress than they need to, and are less likely than expected to experience a full recovery. Every day, interactions with health and care services can waste people's precious time. In addition, taxpayers do not get full value: the productivity benefits that come from effective use of new technology – doing more for less – are not widely realised.'
National Information Board[1]

The consequences of a shortage of analytical expertise are not always obvious or immediately visible. The effects can be hidden in a range of suboptimal decisions and choices based on limited or inappropriate evidence. Some of the areas of health care in which good data analysis is critical are:

*   clinical decision-making

*   innovation and improvement in care

*   board-level oversight of complex organisations and care systems

*   everyday management

*   responding to national initiatives and regulation

*   resource allocation

*   understanding patient flow

*   supporting new data and new digital tools

*   helping patients and the public to use information.

1. To support clinical decision-making

Support for clinical decision-making is one area where new technologies are changing quickly, as evidenced by the proliferation of tools and algorithms to help clinicians diagnose and manage disease. Development is rapid in both the public and private sectors,[10,11,12] and in health care the digital future seems rich with possibility. As Robert Wachter noted, 'Big-data techniques will guide the treatment of individual patients, as well as the best ways to organize our systems of care'.[13]

There is growing interest in the possibilities of 'big data' and artificial intelligence (AI). Although much of this is, for the time being, aspirational, it is clear that such developments will require a skilled workforce that can ensure that tools are implemented in the right way. As noted in the Topol review,[14] development of the workforce is critical for advancements to be fully realised, as staff will need to understand the issues of data validity and accuracy. Indeed, it is possible that the future clinical teams will include data scientists and bio-informaticians.

Some new technologies are already in widespread use: for example, analytical tools such as predictive-risk algorithms that use historical information to make predictions about a future event. These might use patients' electronic records to predict the probability that an individual might suffer an adverse event (such as requiring an emergency admission to hospital). These tools can help clinicians identify where to focus preventive services to avoid acute health problems occurring. Such tools cannot replace clinical judgement, but they might enhance it.

At their best, these predictive tools can operate within existing information systems and seamlessly provide input to a clinical decision. In many cases, they can function as standalone tools. But for the best results they will often require analytical support, which means that using them becomes something more than simply switching on a software module.[15]

So, when applying predictive risk algorithms, several questions need to be considered:

- Are you able to extract the right data from operational systems?

- Can you analyse aggregate patterns across patients?

- Do you need to calibrate predictive models on local data?

- Will the model perform as expected, given the differences in the way information is collected and coded at a local level?

- What are the characteristics of high-risk patients and how can interventions be designed to improve the care they receive?

Other predictive tools are being tested as part of the Health Foundation's Advancing Applied Analytics programme in areas such as general practice and mental health (Boxes 3 and 4).

Box 3: Exploring the use of a frailty measure in general practice

Example from the Health Foundation's Advancing Applied Analytics programme
The Electronic Frailty Index (eFI) uses general-practice read codes to identify frailty in the practice population. It was developed by the National Institute for Health Research Collaboration for Leadership in Applied Health Research and Care in Yorkshire and Humber.

The eFI tool is now available to all general practices in Midlothian. Midlothian Health and Social Care Partnership is running a project that draws on analysis and QI methods to explore how eFI can be used in primary care, and the implications for community health care as well as hospital services. The approach was to consider the whole system to identify all patients with frailty in Midlothian. Support was then provided to general practices to analyse their own data.

Box 4: Applying a risk-prediction tool in mental health settings

Example from the Health Foundation's Advancing Applied Analytics programme
Risk-stratification tools are currently used across the NHS, for example to help identify which general practice patients are at the highest risk of being admitted to hospital. The potential benefits of this are that patients are prevented from experiencing an adverse event and emergency-care costs are avoided.

Birmingham and Solihull Mental Health NHS Foundation Trust is applying risk stratification to mental health by building models that predict the likelihood of an individual being admitted to psychiatric hospital. The aim is to develop and implement a risk-stratification model that will help clinicians prevent mental-health patients from requiring urgent hospital care. The model uses 4 years of historical clinical and sociodemographic data to provide an overall indication of the risk of a patient experiencing a mental health crisis. The data is drawn from a range of sources and is not limited to a set of patient characteristics such as age, diagnosis and previous hospital admissions.

The project looks at how the models can be used in practice, working with a number of the Trust's community mental-health teams to pilot the risk-stratification model. Analysts will work with clinicians and managers to refine, test, implement and see how they can embed it into systems for routine clinical care. The goal is to understand its impact on clinical decision-making and make improvements as part of a continuous cycle of learning via a comprehensive evaluation process.

2. To support innovation and improvement in care

The NHS is awash with innovations designed to deliver 'better' care, triggered by a desire to improve quality of care, the need for financial solvency, or both.[16] Examples include integrated models of care, digital-first approaches to primary care, new algorithms to detect diseases, and the establishment of rapid diagnostic services to detect cancers. Despite the hunger for innovation, however, there is often no way to know whether these changes will actually improve care (eg around reducing emergency admissions).[17,18,19]

While traditional evaluation can help understand what works, the process can also be too slow or too restrictive, requiring the process of care to remain unchanged until the study has been completed (or allowing only for small changes). What is needed is an approach to monitoring the effects of innovation in close to real time, so that teams (local or national) can 'course correct' along the way. An example of such an evaluation model is given in Box 5.

These evaluations can reveal higher-quality care, such as a recent evaluation from the Improvement Analytics Unit. It found that residents of care homes who received enhanced support experienced 23% fewer emergency admissions than expected.[20] Even when an evaluation reveals that the intervention has not delivered the gains that were anticipated, it still produces valuable learning. In a complex environment, not every change will produce the intended effect and it is important to identify where the results were not as expected.

Box 5: Improvement Analytics Unit and NHS vanguard local evaluation[21]

The Improvement Analytics Unit is an innovative partnership between NHS England and the Health Foundation. It provides rapid feedback on whether progress is being made by local health care projects that focus on improving care and efficiency in England.

Robust statistical methods are used by the unit to evaluate local initiatives and interventions in health care, such as those being delivered as part of major national programmes (eg the integrated care systems). The unit aims to provide rapid feedback to local services and decision-makers to enable them to improve care.

The unit assesses whether the care outcomes for patients covered by the new initiatives are different in any significant way from the outcomes of patients who are not part of the initiative. The unit's analysis will inform ongoing learning and improvement. This analysis can be combined with intelligence at a local level, guiding the development of improvement projects and change to services on the ground.

Implementing new approaches to the delivery of services can be challenging and take considerable time and effort from front-line teams. If these teams are going to have the best chance of improving patient care, they need better analytical support to help them understand the effects of their work to date and make improvements.

Questions that recur when supporting change are whether and how to provide help to clinical and managerial teams. It is often done using external consultants, but the downsides, apart from the initial expense, include the fact that the consultants' skills and expertise are not transferred to the internal teams. The newly achieved solutions may not be sustainable. In 2016, the board of Taunton and Somerset NHS Foundation Trust took the bold step of making a big investment in developing permanent, internal improvement capability: creating the right culture, structure, tools and processes to enable and empower their workforce to improve from within. The decision was prompted by a concern that the use of external consultants had proved too costly and unsustainable. As a result, the Trust has successfully minimised spend on external consultants and now has a thriving team within the organisation to support improvement work. Box 6 outlines the model they have adopted.

Box 6: Developing in-house capability to support change[22]

Taunton and Somerset NHS Foundation Trust
Historically, Taunton and Somerset NHS Foundation Trust's approach was to use external 'experts' and management consultants to bolster the Trust's ability to deliver improvement. This was costly and unsustainable. The results and benefits that promised were not always delivered, measured or sustained. The 'experts' the Trust worked with each had their own approach, tools and processes for delivering change. Projects often operated in organisational silos. There was no single, clear picture of improvement projects across the Trust and accountability between projects was inconsistent.

Staff at the Trust mapped the current structure of improvement projects, who was working on them and where they reported. This generated a proliferation of boards, steering groups and projects. They quickly realised that the Trust needed to radically rethink how it implemented improvement if it wanted to survive and thrive.

The Trust's model

Based on internal data and mapping, as well as evidence of what had worked elsewhere, staff at the Trust proposed a new structure for improvement, comprising five elements:

1. A proprietary 'blended' methodology that combines proven Institute for Health Improvement methodology with project management and benefits realisation. This blended approach is designed to ensure effective governance and monitoring of projects, and to drive out and capture project benefits.

2. A dedicated improvement team with the technical skills and experience to partner with and coach clinical and operational teams to deliver improvement projects in their areas. The improvement team is centrally financed and structurally detached, and is focused on delivering results at the organisational level.

3. A governance structure of clinician-led 'improvement boards' based on 'constant' themes within the hospital.

4. A comprehensive and ambitious training plan to equip individuals and teams with the skills they need to improve their part of the organisation using Institute for Healthcare Improvement methodology.

5. An evidence-based approach to improvement, ensuring that the Trust leverages the experience and best practice of others and proactively shares its own learning.

3. To facilitate board-level oversight of complex organisations and care systems

'IT and information is the ownership of the board and the senior management, if they're not using it to run their organisation they're in the wrong job. There is nothing more complicated than running the NHS and if we don't do it as smart as any organisation in the world then we're really betraying the taxpayer and we're betraying our patients.'
Matthew Swindells[23]

Good-quality information and intelligence is critical for a board to be effective. Box 7 gives an example from a study looking at the quality of care. A study of NHS providers suggested that one of the key elements in achieving successful provider transformation is insight from data analysis that enables a fact-based understanding of problems, informed decision-making and performance-tracking.[24]

The task of organising complex information and presenting it in ways that are meaningful and relevant to board-level decision-makers should be one of the fundamental roles of the analysts. However, in many cases, reporting at board level falls short of what is required and relies on long, unprocessed lists of tables. Sometimes, the problem is not a shortage of information but rather an 'overabundance of irrelevant information'.[25]

One study looking at how boards work on improving the quality of care ranked organisations in terms of the maturity of their approach to quality improvement (QI). They found that organisations with high levels of QI maturity received reports in which the data were clear and readable, and in which different sources of data were discussed together (eg data on staffing levels considered alongside data on staff wellbeing and patient experience). By contrast, reports to boards with low levels of QI maturity were characterised by a large volume of data, which was often not clearly presented, reviewed in silos and not linked to improvement actions.[26]

An experienced NHS manager observed that 'the NHS gathers a massive amount of data but largely fails to use it intelligently. Energy is misplaced … most is spent downloading and gathering data, followed by preparing reports, analysing data, and ultimately using the data to make decisions'.[25]

A recurring issue is how board-level reports handle statistical uncertainty. Most measurement contains some degree of uncertainty arising from chance variation and basic statistical methods; this is a widely accepted way to distinguish a systematic trend from an ambiguous one. Yet one study found that of a total of 1,488 charts found in board reports, only 6% acknowledged the role of chance.[27] This presents a risk that boards react to changes in metrics that are the result of chance and do not reflect any real change to the underlying care processes – wasting time and resources. One approach to addressing these problems is to move from Red Amber Green ratings to statistical process control charts, as suggested by NHS Improvement in the initiative Making Data Count.[28]

Box 7: Analysing quality at the organisational level

To improve the quality of care and identify risk in the system, it is important that high-quality intelligence is available to teams across the organisation. One study of hospital boards found this could vary widely, despite organisations 'putting considerable time, effort and resources into data collection and monitoring systems'.[29]

The study report describes how the better organisations typically used a variety of data sources: routinely collected data, data collection initiatives, and other sources like spot checks and audits. However, there were significant differences between organisations in how effectively that data was turned into 'actionable knowledge' and organisational response. Some organisations used information to detect issues (problem-sensing behaviour), while others used information less usefully to provide reassurance (comfort-seeking behaviour).

'Problem-sensing involved actively seeking out weaknesses in organisational systems, and it made use of multiple sources of data—not just mandated measures, but also softer intelligence […] Senior teams displaying problem-sensing behaviours tended to be cautious about being self-congratulatory; perhaps more importantly, when they did uncover problems, they often used strategies that went beyond merely sanctioning staff at the sharp end, making more holistic efforts to strengthen their organisations and teams.'[29]

4. To improve everyday management

In terms of basic operational management, there are many opportunities for good analysis to make everyday tasks more efficient. New software tools allow better reporting and allow managers and clinicians to access information closer to where the decisions get made.[30] Examples include Qlik, Tableau and Beautiful Information (Box 8).*

Wrightington, Wigan and Leigh NHS Financial Trust has developed a suite of analytical apps that support the organisation and its provision of healthcare from ward to board. Their most renowned app supports their A&E department in monitoring demand (both current and predicted), wait times, decisions to admit and other aspects of patient flow.

---

* For more information, go to www.qlik.com, www.tableau.com/learn/webinars/transforming-healthcare-data-insight or http://beautifulinformation.org/solutions/performance

The app has become the 'single version of the truth' and supports both the department and the Trust executives in their decision-making. Since its introduction, the app has helped reduce the median length of stay by 30 minutes: improving discharge levels, reducing delays and minimising readmissions. Although the app may look simple, it contains complex algorithms that use things like weather data to determine how many people are likely to turn up at A&E in the hours and days ahead.

The Trust has developed other apps that support the organisation's referral-to-treatment times, theatre efficiency, budget management, outpatient and inpatient care, and monitoring of variations in care.

Mark Singleton, Associate Director of Information Management and Technology for the Trust, said 'We are so lucky to have such as a fabulous Business Intelligence team that have developed a recipe for success when it comes to working with Clinical Services and producing ground-breaking apps that support the organisation in so many different ways but ultimately to ensure the organisation provides the best care for its patients.'*

Box 8: Example of an information tool for managers[31]

Operational Control Centre
- A web-based app available on any smartphone, tablet or desktop platform.
- Provides aggregated, real-time data.
- A proactive management tool that highlights bed capacity and delays in the system.
- Available anytime and anywhere, in the hospital or off-site.
- Control over access to unlimited users.
- Developed by Beautiful Information, an NHS/private partnership.

---
*   M Singleton, personal communication, 2019.

Data analytics have also been beneficial to commissioners (Box 9).

Box 9: Using data analytics to support better commissioning decisions.[32]

Bradford Districts Clinical Commissioning Group used the three-stage RightCare methodology (where to look, what to change, how to change) to focus on clinical programmes and identify value opportunities. They employed evidence-based methods with a clear emphasis on outcomes to inform the commissioning and delivery of programmes to improve heart health.

In its first year of operation, Bradford's Healthy Hearts helped 14,000 patients in the Bradford area and has already potentially prevented 50 heart attacks and 50 strokes. More than 960 people in the Bradford area are now on vital stroke-preventing medicine, which has reduced the risk of stroke by up to 75% in these patients, and avoided nearly 88 devastating strokes a year. This is an anticoagulation rate of nearly 82%, the highest in the region. Over 4,500 patients at moderate to high risk of heart attack and stroke have been prescribed statins to reduce their risk. By switching to different statins, over 6,000 patients have reduced their cholesterol level. The risk of stroke for people with atrial fibrillation has been reduced by more than two-thirds by anticoagulant medication prescribed by a doctor.

5. To better respond to national initiatives and regulation

The local health and care agenda is often shaped by external demands from national government and arm's-length bodies (Box 10). These will typically have a framework for accountability and performance assessment that is applied to local providers and commissioners of care. The tools used as the basis for these performance assessments frequently rely on complex analytical methods when defining performance targets or metrics, such as the Summary Hospital Mortality Index. Very often, local analytical teams are needed to interpret these national information measures and put them into local context.

For example, as part of the annual planning round, providers are obliged to generate demand forecasts for their key points of delivery (eg emergency admissions, outpatient referrals). For many organisations, these forecasts have been relatively naive in construction, ignoring core concepts like trends and seasonality. To bridge the gap and generate good-quality returns, NHS Improvement decided to develop univariate-time-series forecasting tools to help providers increase the level of sophistication and statistical rigour of their forecasts. The tools and outputs developed were delivered at scale using web-based interfaces and dedicated output files. The code driving the tools was developed on an open-source platform. It could then be shared with local analysts, who could re-use and amend it as necessary. This univariate-forecasting approach is now a standardised methodology for both NHS Improvement and NHS England.

It can be difficult for an individual organisation to ignore some of the approaches developed by national bodies, such as NHS England or the Care Quality Commission, when these are used in performance management or regulatory discussions. An organisation without sufficient analytical capability will be at a distinct disadvantage in such discussions.[33]

Box 10: How government requirements and expectations can shape how data analysis is used within a service

Performance measurement and targets

For some time, a system of nationally mandated indicators and targets has been a national tool for driving policy changes. Interpreting changes in these indicators is often a more complex process than a superficial analysis suggests.

Population health management

As part of *The NHS Long Term Plan*, the NHS 'will deploy population health management solutions to support [integrated care systems] to understand the areas of greatest health need and match NHS services to meet them'.[3] Analytical methods such as population segmentation and impactibility modelling are key, and integrated care systems will need to be able to use them effectively.

Case-mix analysis

The increasingly complex language of healthcare resource groups has been used for almost 20 years in funding acute care. A fairly basic scheme has seen a variety of refinements and adaptions to incentivise changes to care.

Patient and staff surveys

Established as a national requirement some years ago and still one of the most commonly used comparative performance tools.

Understanding mortality differences

Over the past decade, the monitoring of hospital fatality rates has been the subject of intense national and local debate.[34,35,36] However, a number of local organisations had begun to monitor hospital mortality rates; government interest following the Francis report added momentum to work on standardised measures, such as the Summary Hospital-level Mortality Indicator.[37]

Variation in care and GIRFT

More recently, initiatives such as RightCare and Getting it Right First Time (GIRFT) have used a combination of centralised analysis to develop benchmarking data that local organisations cannot generate themselves and support to interpret and analyse the implications for the local context.

6. To better allocate resources

Moving resource allocation from simply reinforcing historical funding patterns to a system that represents need has been a recurrent theme in health policy since the 1960s.[38] It is an area in which local interests battle hard for their share of the pot, and one where good analytical support is essential to understanding the evidence and weigh different arguments.

At a national level, the analysis can be complex and often involves expert teams advising on government strategies. As the National Audit Office noted, 'Given the amount of money involved – equivalent to nearly £1,400 per person each year – the way in which the Department [of Health and Social Care] and NHS England allocate funding to local commissioners is a crucial part of the way the health system works. These decisions are complex, involving mathematical formulae and elements of judgement.'[39]

There is some evidence that national policy of resource allocation had an impact on reducing inequalities between areas. Between 2001 and 2011, the proportion of resources allocated to deprived areas in England compared with that allocated to more affluent areas was associated with a reduction in absolute health inequalities from causes amenable to good health care.[40]

Aside from the implementation of national allocation methods, there is also a need for better analysis to support ways to identify local priorities in allocating resources. As Geraldine Strathdee, Chair of the National Mental Health Intelligence Network, noted, without benchmarking data, NHS resources are allocated on the basis of historical patterns, guesswork or the 'loudest voice'.[41]

7. To understand patient flow

The past few years have seen a recognition of the importance of understanding the way patients flow through the care system.[42] Often, the best way to achieve that is through the use of sophisticated methods such as modelling, yet their uptake has been patchy.

Good examples do exist: for example, work to understand demand for long-term care in Kent (Box 11). Others have used tools such as simulation and queueing theory to look at scheduling community mental-health assessments.[43] In Sheffield, local teams have applied simulation modelling to evaluate the reconfiguration of stroke services in Sheffield and South Yorkshire and this work has been integral to decision-making.

The challenge in adopting these tools routinely has been linked to a lack of capacity in health services; too few staff members are felt to have the training or ability to use the models.[44] This is especially relevant considering current concerns with managing urgent and emergency care and flows.[45,46]

Box 11: Modelling demand for long-term care[47]

The Kent public health team began supporting the Kent and Medway Primary Care Trust cluster with the local Long Term Conditions Year of Care Commissioning Programme in 2012. At the time, there was limited understanding of how to quantify and estimate the benefits of the Quality, Innovation, Productivity and Prevention (QIPP) 'long term conditions' model of care on the wider Kent health economy, other than high-level national evidence. Intelligence and analysis of service use within integrated care models focused on the effects on individual organisations, but did not reflect wider patient journeys across all care settings. The aim of the public-health, whole-population approach was to create a baseline profile of how individuals with complex care needs affect hospital services during periods of crisis, alongside their use of other services, compared with other individuals.

The information is being used to model demand for services and to assess the impact of service-change interventions across the whole health and care system. Analysis and dashboard metrics have been referenced in several key needs-assessment documents and other strategic plans. For example, a recent evaluation of a falls-prevention service by a community health provider used a linked, whole-population community health and hospital dataset to examine falls-related admissions before and after patients were referred to the falls service. This enabled a more sophisticated evaluation of whether the change in trends might actually be caused by patients using the new service.

The Health Foundation has been promoting local work to look at patient flow through the service. One recent review of a flow training programme in Wales noted the challenges of accessing the analytical time needed to support this work: 'Another substantial constraint was that none of the local health boards had sufficient capacity and expertise in data collection and analysis to provide ongoing support to clinicians and make sure they had the right information in the right format for effective decision-making.'[48]

8. To support new data and new digital tools

Another reason to support analytical capability is that it could open the way to new data-driven technologies, for example machine-learning algorithms and AI, that could help with the diagnosis and management of health conditions. Data are essential to the development of these technologies, and the NHS has some of the best health care data in the world. *The NHS Long Term Plan* envisages a role for private-sector companies, with an aim to 'encourage a world leading health IT industry in England with a supportive environment for software developers and innovators'.[3] Successful delivery of this innovation agenda is likely to depend on joint working between NHS teams and industry. NHS analytical teams have a lot to contribute in this area. They understand how NHS data are being collected and why, and they can act as a valuable bridge between NHS clinicians and managers and data scientists in industry.

To take advantage of new methods, analysts must have access to the right software tools, particularly open-source programming tools that allow analysts to learn from each other (eg R and Python). In the early 2000s, open-source software began to gain acceptance, even among the sceptics. Today, open-source software is practically embedded in large, commercial organisations such as Facebook, Google, Twitter and banking and blue-chip corporations. They are taking full advantage and seeing the benefits of its power and scale. Some, such as Facebook, are actively developing and sharing their software tools within the wider open-source community, and some of those tools have been embraced in health care (eg Prophet[49]).

The NHS has been much slower in accepting and seeing the value of open-source software, although the Department of Health and Social Care has recently announced that the newly created NHSX will ensure that all source code is open by default.[50] One of the main barriers to wider deployment of open-source tools has been the reluctance of IT staff to install open-source software on secure health care systems. One analytics manager confided: 'Getting an open-source application installed on my NHS laptop was a lengthy and arduous process. IT professionals were particularly risk averse to deploy software on their systems especially given the highly sensitive information they contain. We battled with the reluctance because we saw the value add it would give us. Now the software is installed, we are starting to realise the value add, why it's so popular, and the awesome things it can do – you can see the reason why all the big organisations have embraced it. We are doing some things very differently now, it has allowed us to work more on our methodologies rather than churn.'*

---

* P. Stroner, personal communication, 2019.

Open-source tools such as 'R', a statistical programme that is gaining recognition in commercial and public-sector applications, present an opportunity. Open-source offerings include generalised tools such as Python (used as the platform for GCSE computing) as well as niche analytical disciplines such as JaamSim (used for discrete-event simulation). Open-source tools enable analysts to explore and sample an array of new analytical tools and techniques they can ultimately deploy in their organisations. The challenge for the future is to take advantage of these exciting analytical tools by building analytical capability. This includes the networks needed to allow collaboration, such as the NHS-R Community (Box 12).

Box 12: How open-source software tools can support better analysis in health care

The NHS-R Community was established in 2017 with an Applied Analytics Award from the Health Foundation. It is an online and face-to-face community dedicated to promoting the learning, application and use of the open-source 'R' tool in the NHS in the UK.

One key aspect of this project was the way analysts can share resources (typically code) and expertise, and so improve analytical capability in the system. Moreover, the network had stimulated a wider conversation about what analysts can contribute to health care and the features of high-performing analytical teams. This is the kind of cross-organisational collaboration that the Health Foundation is seeking to encourage.

The NHS-R Community has so far achieved:

- a dedicated website (https://nhsrcommunity.com)
- delivery of problem-oriented workshops in Wales and Yorkshire
- the 2018 NHS-R Community Conference to promote the use of R in the NHS, which was attended by 119 delegates from across the UK and Europe.

The UK government, in its Life Sciences Industrial Strategy,[51] sees health-service data as being of value to those developing new digital tools. For example, the Open Prescribing project[52] uses existing data streams on prescribing collected from GP practices by NHS Digital. The raw data files are huge, with more than 700 million rows, so a team at Oxford have put together some analytical tools that are freely available to GPs, managers and the public.[52]

Over the coming years, NHS organisations may wish to provide private companies with access to NHS data, for example to help with the development of new algorithms or drugs. The benefit for the NHS might include seconded data scientists working alongside NHS teams. In that situation, we'd recommend an emphasis on skills transfer, so that the NHS builds its capability to conduct analysis in a sustainable way.

9. To help patients and the public use information

Investing in data analytics enables new information flows to and from patients and the general public.[53] This information can help people make better-informed decisions about their care, as well as contribute more effectively to the development of their local services. There are also opportunities to engage the public in decisions about how data are used.

Table 2 lists some of the ways in which these information flows operate. Although many revolve around the use of new technological tools, it is important to recognise that there is still a significant analytical role in reporting, presenting and understanding the data.

Table 2: How analysts can support information-sharing

Flow of information	Role of analysts
Sharing information about performance and running of health services	Organising and presenting information on organisational performance in accessible and easily interpreted ways (eg websites).
Applying tools to discover patients' views on the quality of services	The design and analysis of questionnaires and other tools to assess patient experience and satisfaction with services. It is important to do this well – there are many examples of poorly conducted or analysed questionnaires in use.
Applying tools that capture aspects of a person's health or wellbeing (eg smartphone apps)	A person's perception of their own wellbeing is widely accepted as an outcome measure and there are a range of tools to explore this. New technology is also growing to enable people to record information about their health. Choosing and using the right instrument and correctly interpreting derived data is an important analytical role.
Information flows between new monitoring tools and telehealth	The use of remote monitoring of health information is seen as increasingly important in the management of chronic illness. It also finds its way into many people's everyday lives. But there are still challenges in how this information flows through health care systems at an individual or aggregate level, and there are ways that its power can be exploited.
Engaging patients and the population in decisions about health services and delivery	The challenge here is to help summarise information in a way that can help the public understand how the health care system works. This means selecting which information is used and how it is best presented so that it is both accurate and easily understood.
Helping manage information about patients' experiences of care	Information from patients about their experiences of care has come to be recognised as a key dimension in understanding the quality of care. The design, administration and interpretation of such tools need to be undertaken with caution. For example, survey results are often presented in meaningless rankings that do not acknowledge statistical variability and sampling errors.

Do managers underestimate the value of data analysis?

People make decisions under constraints. These might be knowledge constraints or constraints imposed by analytical ability. Decision-making is therefore based on heuristics: experience-based techniques for problem-solving, or 'knowing by trying'. The 'recognition heuristic' is when people make a decision based on only one piece of information, recognition – the knowledge that many others have chosen the same option.[54]

Analytical input can be considered too slow, misguided or irrelevant to the problem at hand. The divide between analyst and senior manager can be further widened by:

- The challenge of choosing the right analytical approach to fit the managerial problem. This is partly an issue of whether analysts have effective communication skills. It is also a question of whether analytical teams have the skills to unpick problems and questions from senior managers in ways that match the analysis they can do. This is an area in which external management consultants often excel.

- Expectations of what constitutes good (enough) analysis. If senior managers have little experience in data analysis, they may not be able to recognise the value that data analysis can bring and the difference that it can make.

One way to bridge the divide is to invest in people who span professional boundaries. In our previous report, *Understanding analytical capability in health care: Do we have more data than insight?*, many interviewees described the importance of analytical leadership, in particular people who understand the possibilities that good analysis can engender (and how analytical teams work), yet who can also engage with managers at the highest levels to influence and shape demand for analysis.[7] Organisations with a well-developed analytical workforce also tend to have strong leaders who are influential within the organisation, whether these are chief analysts or in Chief Information Officer roles, and in some cases they may be strong clinical professionals. The implication is that enhancing the profile of good-quality analytics within an organisation must involve recognising the current generation of leaders as well as investing in the next generation. A key skill is to spot opportunities for analysis that other senior staff don't see, and manage expectations around requests for analysis.

The right presence at the organisation's decision-making level can help shift the relationship between decision-makers and their in-house analytical teams. The direction of change is from a relationship where the analysts unquestioningly provide whatever they have been asked to provide, to one where the requests received will address the problems and begin to be anticipated, and to an extent shaped, by the analytical team (Box 13).

Box 13: What does a health service with a strong analytical component look like?

- Both the provider and the commissioner of care have some understanding of the outcomes, costs and quality of care they offer. More important still is that they constantly test how changes in the organisation of service are affecting patients and populations.

- Existing health service data are widely used. The data are easily and securely accessible, actively curated and renowned for accuracy and utility. Individual organisations have ways to link new data streams to existing patient records to expand the overall understanding of quality and effectiveness throughout patient journeys over time.

- Clinicians and managers rely on a range of analytical tools to understand local performance and quality. They can access expert commentary and advice on interpreting such data and initiate new analyses.

- A thriving analytical community in which new developments and methods are actively shared between organisations. There is a role and career structure that is attractive to new graduates and that retains the best people, developing them into senior analytical roles.

- Where analytical teams, with the provider and the commissioner, can access expertise from academia and the industry to help them solve problems and implement new methods of working. Opportunities exist for changing career paths from a specialist data scientist to an analyst working in the service (and vice versa).

- The boards of major organisations exploit the right analytical methods to support their deliberations. For example, analysis of change over time replaces static Red Amber Green ratings, performance is assessed using valid comparators, statistical uncertainty is recognised and data are interpreted in context. Board-level reports are succinct and focused on the most important issues, yet capable of supporting an understanding of quality of care.

- Major changes in service, delivery and innovations in care are designed with input from analytical teams from the start, and are accompanied by evaluation programmes to help with further course correction.

- The publication and dissemination of information about health-service performance does some justice to the complexity of health care delivery. The media reports focus on substantive issues, not coincidences in data.

- The public can access and understand a range of comparative information about health care delivery, which helps them play a greater part in their own care and in shaping services more generally.

- Information about the wider determinants of population health is routinely used to shape decisions about investment.

- Senior managers and clinicians have developed a full understanding of where better analytics are needed in their organisation and address these in their local workforce plans.

- The public and patients are engaged in conversations on how data are used. There is broad public support for how the NHS uses data and individuals can opt out of data-sharing.

How can we address the shortfall in analytical capability?

The shortfall in analytical capability has been growing for some time. It would be over-optimistic to think there were simple, short-term solutions to address that. As with most things, we need to see action at several levels and over sustained periods. The following areas are particularly important.

What can be done at the national level?

- **Invest in analysts working in support of the service.** There are several ways in which the role of analysis can be recognised and developed. There are some good existing programmes, but coverage is patchy. *The NHS Long Term Plan*[3] places a strong emphasis on the benefits of new technology but investment in skilled analysis must be on par with investment in technologies. We need clearer statements about the importance of analytical capability and support for organisations working on analytical career development.

- **Develop a strategy for developing analytical capability.** Given the importance of good-quality analytics for supporting quality and efficiency improvements, as well as innovation in the NHS, a comprehensive strategy for building analytical capability is required. This should address the current limitations (set out in Box 2).

- **Place a much stronger emphasis on translational analytics.** Academic institutes have invested significantly in data science. This investment needs to be complemented by approaches that bridge the gap between academic research and real-life practice. Funding bodies should provide incentives for the implementation and spread of new analytical methods.

- **Set expectations for what is appropriate analysis for supporting key decisions.** Many existing national initiatives aim to improve the quality and efficiency of the health care service, and they often place demands on local analytical teams to provide data or conduct analyses. Arm's-length bodies have an opportunity to improve the quality of analytics by raising the expectations of what data analysis is appropriate. It is important to allow for flexibility, so that local analytical teams can properly work with clinical teams and managers to understand the problem and apply appropriate analytical methods.

- **Provide opportunities for analytical teams to share learning.** The analytical community is currently very fragmented, with limited opportunities for teams to share learning. National bodies can help overcome these problems by developing a learning infrastructure as part of national programmes. This could take the form of websites and conferences that allow analysts to share their challenges and support each other. These initiatives can complement those that the analytical community develops for itself.

- **Support programmes aimed at clarifying skills, competencies and career frameworks.** Several groups are already looking to develop more consistent frameworks to describe analytical skills and competencies. This work can help recruitment and career development for analysts.

What can local system organisational leaders do?

- **Recognise that analytical capability is a key element of local strategies.** These strategies could relate to information, service transformation or workforce and organisational development.

- **Recognise the need for local analytical capability when implementing new information tools** (such as predictive analytical tools to understand the potential future demand implications of organisational care delivery).

- **Support local training and networking initiatives.** In particular, look for training programmes that work across teams and across organisations. The Health Foundation has some examples of these in our Advancing Applied Analytics awards. We also recommend learning approaches that seek common solutions to shared problems – for example, building robust, validated, locally configurable capacity, demand and patient-flow models to add greater consistency and transparency to decision-making. This process would need to build on well-established methodologies to ensure variation and uncertainty are accounted for. It is important to recognise that training is not just about keeping up with the latest coding or software tools.

- **Audit internal capability and explore what skills and talent already exist in the organisation.** There is a need for more general tools that will help organisations assess their own capability and draw up local plans. Trust boards need to develop themselves to be digitally ready to competently digest good-quality analytical insights and, ultimately, make good decisions.

- **When negotiating partnerships with the private sector, look for opportunities to develop analytical capability.** Over the coming years, NHS organisations may wish to provide private companies with access to NHS data. In return, the private sector could facilitate skills transfer so that the NHS can build analytical capability in a sustainable way.

- **Support and develop people who can work across analytical and senior management/clinical roles.**

- **Work across organisational boundaries to make the most of analytical capability.** This includes investing in the use of linked data to give an overarching view of wider-population health delivery, patient experience and outcomes.

What can the analytical community do?

- **Exploit opportunities for networking, sharing learning, collaborating and sharing analyst-developed tools that have cross-organisation use.** The open-source platform lends itself well to this.

- **Invest in personal development:**

    - offered by national bodies (eg NHS Leadership Academy, NHS Digital Academy, Health Education England)

    - delivered by analytical networks/organisations (eg the Association of Professional Healthcare Analysts, NHS-R Community or Academic Health Science Networks).

- **Advocate for itself and not rely on national leadership.** This could mean advocating the benefits of better analysis and being forceful about the business benefits that can accrue.

- **Build teams with a range of analytical skills and find ways to link these with key problems.** Give analysts the opportunity to visit key problem areas to get a better understanding of the analytical techniques required. Help them integrate into wider teams and share the concepts of analytics with clinical colleagues.

- **Recognise the importance of communicating effectively and engaging with senior managers and clinicians about the value of better analysis.** There needs to be an acknowledgement by analysts that the supporting narrative around analysis is an integral part of its delivery. It's not just the numbers!

- **Develop better ways to select the right analytical approach for a given problem.** This is an area where analytical networks can add real value, enabling analysts to seek peer support, access expert opinion and draw from the experience of others in their community in relative safety.

References

1. National Information Board. *Personalised Health and Care 2020: Using Data and Technology to Transform Outcomes for Patients and Citizens. A Framework for Action.* National Information Board, 2014 (www.digitalhealth.net/includes/images/news0254/PDF/0172_NHS_England_NIB_Report_WITH_ADDITIONAL_MATERIAL_S8.pdf).

2. NHS England. *Digital Transformation* [webpage]. NHS England (www.england.nhs.uk/digitaltechnology).

3. NHS England. *The NHS Long Term Plan*. Department of Health and Social Care, 2019.

4. Huesch MD, Mosher TJ. Using it or losing it? The case for data scientists inside health care. *New England Journal of Medicine*. 4 May 2017 (https://catalyst.nejm.org/case-data-scientists-inside-health-care).

5. NHS Confederation. *NHS Statistics, Facts and Figures* [webpage]. NHS Confederation. 14 July 2017 (www.nhsconfed.org/resources/key-statistics-on-the-nhs).

6. NHS England. *Our 2015/16 Annual Report: Health and High Quality Care for All, Now and For Future Generations*. TSO (The Stationery Office), 2016.

7. Bardsley M. *Understanding Analytical Capability in Health Care: Do We Have More Data Than Insight?* Health Foundation; 2016.

8. Farr M. *Down and out in Manchester and Liverpool* [webpage]. Beautiful Information. 14 June 2018 (http://beautifulinformation.org/news/developing-an-information-strategy).

9. Buchan J, Charlesworth A, Gershlick B, Seccombe I. *A Critical Moment: NHS Staffing Trends, Retention and Attrition*. Health Foundation, 2019.

10. Administrative Data Taskforce. *Improving Access for Research and Policy*. The UK Administrative Data Research Network, 2012 (https://esrc.ukri.org/research/our-research/administrative-data-research-network/administrative-data-taskforce-adt).

11. Beresford M. *Demystifying Data: The Data Revolution and What it Means for Local Government*. New Local Government Network, 2015 (www.nlgn.org.uk/public/wp-content/uploads/DEMYSTIFYING-DATA2.pdf).

12. Nesta. *Analytic Britain: Securing the Right Skills for the Data-driven Economy*. Nesta, 2015.

13. Wachter R. *The Digital Doctor: Hope, Hype and Harm at the Dawn of Medicine's Computer Age*. McGraw Hill, 2015.

14. Health Education England. *The Topol Review: Preparing the Healthcare Workforce to Deliver the Digital Future*. Health Education England, 2019.

15. Lewis G, Curry N, Bardsley M. *Choosing a Predictive Risk Model: A Guide for Commissioners in England*. The Nuffield Trust, 2011.

16. NHS Improvement. *Single Oversight Framework for NHS Providers* [webpage]. NHS Improvement (https://improvement.nhs.uk/resources/single-oversight-framework/).

17. Bardsley M, Steventon A, Smith J, Dixon J. *Evaluating Integrated and Community-Based Care: How Do We Know What Works?* Nuffield Trust, 2013.

18. Purdy S, Paranjothy P, Huntley A, Thoma R, Mann M et al. *Interventions to Reduce Unplanned Hospital Admission: A Series of Systematic Reviews.* University of Bristol, 2012.

19. Lloyd T. *Why Before-and-After Analyses Can Give Misleading Results* [webpage]. Health Foundation. 28 September 2018 (www.health.org.uk/newsletter-feature/why-before-and-after-analyses-can-give-misleading-results).

20. Lloyd T, Wolters A, Steventon A. *The Impact of Providing Enhanced Support for Care Home Residents in Rushcliffe*. Health Foundation, 2017.

21. Health Foundation. *Improvement Analytics Unit* [webpage]. Health Foundation, 2019 (www.health.org.uk/funding-and-partnerships/our-partnerships/improvement-analytics-unit).

22. Gibbons A. *Transforming How We Deliver Improvement Projects at Taunton and Somerset NHS Foundation Trust* [webpage]. The Academy of Fabulous Stuff, 2018 (https://fabnhsstuff.net/fab-stuff/transforming-how-we-deliver-improvement-projects-at-taunton-and-somerset-nhs-foundation-trust).

23. Swindells M. *The Importance of Digital Health in the Implementation of the NHS Five Year Forward View* [video transcript]. The King's Fund, 6 July 2016 (www.kingsfund.org.uk/audio-video/matthew-swindells-digital-health-nhs-five-year-forward-view).

24. McKinsey Hospital Institute. *Transformational Change in NHS Providers*. Health Foundation, 2015.

25. Ackoff RL. Management misinformation systems. *Management Sciences*. 1967; 14: B147–56.

26. Jones L, Pomeroy L, Robert G, Burnett S, Anderson JE et al. How do hospital boards govern for quality improvement? A mixed methods study of 15 organisations in England. *BMJ Quality and Safety*. 2017; 26: 978–86.

27. Schmidtke KA, Poots AJ, Carpio J, Vlaev I, Kandala N-B et al. Considering chance in quality and safety performance measures: an analysis of performance reports by boards in English NHS trusts. *BMJ Quality and Safety*. 2017; 26: 61–9.

28. NHS Improvement. *Making Data Count*. NHS Improvement; 2018.

29. Dixon-Woods M, Baker R, Charles K, Dawson J, Jerzembek G et al. Culture and behaviour in the English National Health Service: Overview of lessons from a large multimethod study. *BMJ Quality and Safety*. 2014; 23: 106–115.

30. Digital Health. *How Tableau Has Transformed How Our NHS Foundation Trust Uses Data Within 6 Months* [webinar]. Digital Health, 2017 (www.digitalhealth.net/event/how-tableau-has-transformed-how-our-nhs-foundation-trust-uses-data-within-6-months-2).

31. Beautiful Information. *Performance* [webpage]. Beautiful Information, 2018 (http://beautifulinformation.org/solutions/performance).

32. BJC Staff. New series on insights from the Bradford Healthy Hearts project. *British Journal of Cardiology*. 2017; 24: 130.

33. Burnett S, Mendel P, Nunes F, Wiig S, van den Bovenkamp H et al. Using institutional theory to analyse hospital responses to external demands for finance and quality in five European countries. *Journal of Health Services and Research Policy*. 2016; 21: 109–117.

34. Lilford R, Mohammed MA, Spiegelhalter D, Thomson R. Use and misuse of process and outcome data in managing performance of acute medical care: avoiding institutional stigma. *Lancet*. 2004; 363: 1147–54.

35. Hogan H, Zipfel R, Neuburger J, Hutchings A, Darzi A et al. Avoidability of hospital deaths and association with hospital-wide mortality ratios: retrospective case record review and regression analysis. *British Medical Journal*. 2015; 351: h3239.

36. Spiegelhalter D, Sherlaw-Johnson, Bardsley M, Blunt I, Woods C et al. Statistical methods for healthcare regulation: rating, screening and surveillance. *Journal of the Royal Statistical Society Series A*. 2012; 175: 1–47.

37. NHS Digital. *Summary Hospital-level Mortality Indicator (SHMI)* [webpage]. NHS Digital (https://digital.nhs.uk/data-and-information/publications/ci-hub/summary-hospital-level-mortality-indicator-shmi).

38. Gorsky M, Millward G. Resource allocation for equity in the British National Health Service, 1948–89: An Advocacy Coalition Analysis of the RAWP. *Journal of Health Politics, Policy and Law*. 2018; 43: 69–108.

39. National Audit Office. *Department of Health and NHS England, Funding Healthcare: Making Allocations to Local Areas. Report by the Comptroller and Auditor General*. National Audit Office, 2014.

40. Barr B, Bambra C, Whitehead M. The impact of NHS resource allocation policy on health inequalities in England 2001-11: Longitudinal ecological study. *British Medical Journal*. 2014; 348: g3231.

41. Noveck BS. Another NHS crisis looms – an inability to analyse data. *The Guardian*, 8 February 2017.

42. Fillingham D, Jones B, Pereira J. *The Challenge and Potential of Whole System Flow: Improving Flow across Whole Health and Care Systems*. Health Foundation, 2016.

43. MASHnet. *Application of Simulation and Queueing Theory to Scheduling Community Mental Health Assessment (Simulation Study)* [webpage]. MASHnet, 2019 (https://mashnet.info/casestudy/application-of-simulation-and-queuing-theory-to-scheduling-community-mental-health-assessment).

44. Pitt M, Monks T, Crowe S, Vasilaki C. Systems modelling and simulation in health service design, delivery and decision making. *BMJ Quality and Safety*. 2016; 25: 38–45.

45. Brailsford SC, Lattimer VA, Tarnaras P, Turnbull JC. Emergency and on-demand health care: modelling a large complex system. *Journal of the Operational Research Society*. 2004; 55: 34–42.

46. NHS Improvement. *Good Practice Guide: Focus on Improving Patient Flow*. NHS Improvement, 2017.

47. NHS Improving Quality. *Population-Level Commissioning for the Future*. NHS Improving Quality, 2013.

48. Crisp H. *Delivering a National Approach to Patient Flow in Wales: Learning from the 1000 Lives Improvement Patient Flow Programme*. Health Foundation, 2017 (www.health.org.uk/sites/health/files/PatientFlowWales.pdf).

49. Facebook Open Source. *Prophet: Forecasting at Scale*. Facebook, 2018 (https://facebook.github.io/prophet).

50. Department for Health and Social Care. *NHSX: New Joint Organisation for Digital, Data and Technology*. Department for Health and Social Care, 2019.

51. Allred M-L. *What Does the Life Sciences Industrial Strategy Mean for the NHS* [webpage]? Arden & GEM, 2018 (https://www.ardengemcsu.nhs.uk/newsinsight/what-does-life-sciences-industrial-strategy-mean-nhs).

52. OpenPrescribing. *Explore England's Prescribing Data* [webpage]. OpenPrescribing, 2019 (https://openprescribing.net).

53. Castle-Clarke S. *The NHS at 70: What Will New Technology Mean for the NHS and its Patients?* Health Foundation, Institute for Fiscal Studies, The King's Fund, Nuffield Trust, 2018.

54. Williams I, Brown H. *Factors Influencing Decisions of Value in Health Care: A Review of the Literature*. University of Birmingham; 2014 (www.nhsconfed.org/-/media/Confederation/Files/Publications/Documents/DOV_HSMC_Final_report_July_281.pdf).

The Health Foundation is an independent charity committed to bringing about better health and health care for people in the UK.

Our aim is a healthier population, supported by high quality health care that can be equitably accessed. We learn what works to make people's lives healthier and improve the health care system. From giving grants to those working at the front line to carrying out research and policy analysis, we shine a light on how to make successful change happen.

We make links between the knowledge we gain from working with those delivering health and health care and our research and analysis. Our aspiration is to create a virtuous circle, using what we know works on the ground to inform effective policymaking and vice versa.

We believe good health and health care are key to a flourishing society. Through sharing what we learn, collaborating with others and building people's skills and knowledge, we aim to make a difference and contribute to a healthier population.

The Health Foundation
T   +44 (0)20 7257 8000
E   info@health.org.uk
🐦 @HealthFdn
www.health.org.uk